Jake and Jen
in the
Balloon of Do[om]

Written by Chris Bradford

Illustrated by Korky Paul

Collins

"Look! Zebra!" said Jake Jones, the explorer.

Jen, the hot-air balloon pilot, flew low over the wild animals. "That newborn is so cute."

3

"The newborn should stay with the group," said Jake. "There's a lion!"

4

"Let's rescue her," said Jen. She waved her arms to chase the lion away.

5

"HEY!" Jen yelled. But her hand hit
the balloon's burner.

The flame blazed and the blue balloon flew high into the air.

"My suit is stuck!" shrieked Jen. Jake pulled her away.

The suit ripped and part of the burner broke off.

"What now?" Jake asked.

The balloon rocketed up. Jen needed to let some hot air escape.

But she couldn't reach the rope to leak the air out.

Then the burner fell silent. "No fuel!" said Jen.

They were helpless as the wind blew
the balloon along.

A grey shape flew over.
"It's a black-shouldered kite!" grinned Jake.

14

He stopped grinning when the rude kite
pecked a hole.

The balloon burst and flew out of control.

Jake and Jen gripped the balloon's capsule.
"We're doomed!" they screeched.

The balloon crashed down, but Jake and Jen were not wounded.

The crash made the zebra jump in fright ...
and the lion too!

19

Their cat mewed and struck out at their older sibling, Shane. Shane dropped the pin. He stood on it. "Ow!"

Jake and Jen sniggered. "As you popped our balloon, *you* should be the lion's prey!"

After reading

Letters and Sounds: Phase 5

Word count: 236

Focus phonemes: /ai/ ay, ey, a-e /ee/ ie, ea /igh/ i, i-e /oa/ o, ow, ou, o-e /oo/ ue, ui, ew, ou, u-e /oo/ oul

Common exception words: out, there, some, of, to, the, into, pulled, she, he, we, be, said, my, were, when, what, their, our, ask

Curriculum links: Science: Animals, including humans; Geography: Name and locate the world's seven continents

National Curriculum learning objectives: Reading/word reading: read accurately by blending sounds in unfamiliar words containing GPCs that have been taught; read words containing taught GPCs; Reading/comprehension: understand both the books they can already read accurately and fluently and those they listen to by checking that the text makes sense to them as they read, and correcting inaccurate reading; making inferences on the basis of what is being said and done

Developing fluency

- Your child may enjoy hearing you read the book.
- Take turns to read a page. Check that your child uses different voices for the narrator, Jen and Jake, and adds emphasis to exclamations.

Phonic practice

- Ask your child to read these words and sort them into groups according to how the /oo/ sound is spelt:
- blue, group, should, suit, newborn, couldn't
- Focus on how the "l" is not sounded out in some "oul" spellings. Ask your child to sound out:

  shouldered   should   couldn't

Extending vocabulary

- On page 7, the flame **blazed**. Ask your child to think of another word with a similar meaning to **blazed**. (e.g. *shone, glowed*)
- On page 10, the balloon **rocketed** up. Ask your child to think of another word with a similar meaning to **rocketed**. (e.g. *shot, whizzed*)
- Take turns to pick a word and together discuss words with similar meanings.